IMAGES
of America

NEW ORLEANS JAZZ

ON THE COVER: Members of the Preservation Hall Jazz Band pose for a publicity photograph in front of the hall in 1967. They are, from left to right, De De Pierce (cornet), Billie Pierce (piano), Cie Frazer (drums), Louis Nelson (trombone), Narvin Kimball (banjo), and Chester Zardis (bass). (Courtesy of Louisiana State Museum.)

IMAGES
of America

NEW ORLEANS JAZZ

Edward J. Branley

ARCADIA
PUBLISHING

Published by Arcadia Publishing
Charleston, South Carolina

Printed in the United States of America

Library of Congress Control Number: 2013951875

For all general information, please contact Arcadia Publishing:
Telephone 843-853-2070
Fax 843-853-0044
E-mail sales@arcadiapublishing.com
For customer service and orders:
Toll-Free 1-888-313-2665

Visit us on the Internet at www.arcadiapublishing.com

This book is dedicated to the late Marty Hurley, master percussionist
and longtime band director at Brother Martin High School
in Gentilly, along with Dominick Caronna and Chris Bailey,
who succeeded Mr. Hurley as band directors at BMHS.
Thanks to you all for nurturing my son's skills on the trombone.

CONTENTS

ACKNOWLEDGMENTS

Thanks to my editors at Arcadia, Jason Humphrey, for helping me get the ball rolling on the book, and Lydia Rollins, for seeing me through the process, which was always a challenge. My deepest appreciation to Irene Wainwright and the special collections staff of the New Orleans Public Library. Thanks to all the photographers and sources who contributed in making this project successful: Carlos "Froggy" May, Stephanie Schoyer, Robert Avery, JonGunnar Gylfason, Netherlands National Archives, Louisiana State Museum, Library of Congress, Darlene Susco, Derek Bridges, Mark Ghstol, US Marine Corps, and the White House Office of Communications.

Once again, all my love to my wife, Helen, and my boys, Kevin Branley and LTJG Justin Branley, US Navy, who put up with me being distracted while working. Thanks to my friends who encouraged the project, particularly those who joined the book's Facebook page and offered suggestions. All the best to Jenifer Hill, my most wonderful friend, and Melissa Case, for her unique brand of motivation and inspiration. Heartfelt thanks to the staff of P.J.'s Coffee at Clearview Mall for putting up with me while I was writing and researching.

The names of organizations are abbreviated in the courtesy of lines as follows:

Library of Congress (LOC)
Louisiana State Museum (LSM)
National Health Service Corps (NHSC)
National Park Service (NPS)
Netherlands National Archives (NNA)
New Orleans Public Library (NOPL)
State Library of Louisiana (SLL)
University of New Orleans (UNO)
US Marine Corps (USMC)

INTRODUCTION

In New Orleans, we love to say that things are a "gumbo," referring to the wonderful soup that somehow manages to combine many different flavors into the perfect food. It is a cliché, but it often is an excellent metaphor. New Orleans–style jazz is also a blend of many different ingredients, but it does one thing that soup does not normally do for you: it makes you move.

New Orleans music is all about movement. In the French-Spanish Colonial period, soldiers would march in time with bugles and drums. Slaves danced in time with their drums and songs. Sailors would make port in New Orleans, bringing with them chanteys and shipboard instruments. By the middle of the 19th century, the city was a major hub for music and entertainment in North America. Music never left the city through the horrors of the Civil War and the Reconstruction that followed, but once those had passed, the city returned to its status of an entertainment destination.

Music was an important accompaniment to food, wine, and sex as New Orleans approached the 20th century. People wanted—no, they needed—music to help them through many aspects of life, from the dance halls on Saturday night to churches on Sunday morning. Orchestras enabled dancing, and brass bands picked up the tempo in the 1890s.

When Charles "Buddy" Bolden and his contemporaries picked up their horns, though, the music made people move rather than the other way around. That is when jazz was born. Military-style brass music became something else when Bolden added his "big four" syncopation. Feet stomped and hands clapped when piano players and drummers improvised along with the cornets. Suddenly, the tunes on the sheet music did not sound the same twice in a row, as musicians now had license to change things, expand the music, and make people move. Bolden made other musicians want to stop being "legitimate," to let go and explore the sound. His bands were popular in the parks, saloons, and dance halls.

The demand for music that made one move was incredible. Bolden's combo spawned others like Joseph "King" Oliver, John Robichaux, Freddie Keppard, and more to pick up the beat. Teens like Edward "Kid" Ory, known as "Dutt" to family and friends, came in on a train from out in the country to hear these bands at the parks and after baseball games. They took the sounds they heard back with them to the farms and rural communities up the Mississippi River, changing them and making them their own. They would then return on subsequent weekends with their instruments, hoping to get noticed by the bandleaders, joining them for gigs.

There was money to be made playing "jass" and "ragtime" in New Orleans at the turn of the century. (The change in spelling from "jass" to "jazz" is one of the genre's big mysteries, but the word was standardized as "jazz" in print by 1918.) While the new stylings created by Bolden and his contemporaries had not reached the ears of the majority of white folks, there were enough affluent African Americans in the city to nurture musicians along. The sound moved from the bars to a wider audience, one where more white people would hear it. Musicians looking to make the most of their weekend time would parade on the backs of horse-drawn carts, advertising their gigs that evening. White musicians caught the beat, and jazz moved from blacks-only establishments into white bars and onto college campuses. Many whites-only establishments would not even permit African American bands. Segregation presented white musicians with many opportunities, as many whites-only establishments would not even permit black bands.

Life in the segregated South of the early 20th century was tough, not only for musicians but also for all African Americans. As the Great Migration of blacks from the Jim Crow states to northern, industrial cities took place, musicians followed them. Knowing they would find work playing for the black communities in cities like Chicago, bandleaders King Oliver and Kid Ory gave up on hassles of dealing with white saloon owners, police, and patrons who thought they were better than the band in every way. The cream of the crop of New Orleans jazz connected with their counterparts up north and the music spread. Life in Chicago was cold and hard for the men who played Lincoln Park and Storyville, but at least they did not have to sit at the back of the bus on their way home from work.

Improvements in recording technology also spread the gospel of jazz. Instead of the fragile wax cylinders used to record musicians in the 1900s and 1910s, bands were recorded on celluloid and, later, vinyl discs. The advent of electrical recording in the mid-1920s enabled a greater distribution of jazz, as the music industry in New York began to hear players from Chicago without having to get on a train. Jazz might not have been moving mountains, but it was certainly moving millions.

Of course, not all African American musicians abandoned New Orleans for the promises of the northern cities. Bandleaders like Fate Marable negotiated paid gigs on the riverboats, operating locally on daytime excursions, as well as the boats transporting passengers to and from St. Louis. The Creoles of New Orleans continued to demand entertainment, and a new generation of young musicians, those who had heard the fathers of jazz as teens, were now ready to provide the music. The original sounds of King Oliver, Kid Ory, and Louis Armstrong continued in New Orleans even though jazz elsewhere began to evolve into "swing" and the "big band" sound. New Orleanians still liked their "Dixieland" style, even if those playing it did not improvise and experiment as much as their predecessors. Because of that lack of innovation, however, New Orleans faded from jazz prominence as larger cities applied their influence to what had begun here. Depression and war made it difficult for the journeymen musicians to make a living, and people wanted to swing to forget their troubles.

By the late 1940s, the Dixieland players were getting older, and many were only playing at each other's funerals. Realizing that time was short to get some of the original players recorded on vinyl, producers and jazz historians brought the old men onto the stage and into studios. They were interviewed, questioned, and encouraged, and the 1950s revival of the New Orleans sound carried the traditions forward. Local historians and aficionados organized and made commitments: to museums, to recording, and to preservation. People of influence, such as Edmond "Doc" Souchon, worked to develop collections of music, photographs, and memorabilia. Though funding was often difficult, they could always lean on the old men to do benefit concerts. Larry Borenstein's arguably selfish desire to hear traditional jazz music while he ran his French Quarter art studio turned out to be a miracle for the movement, as it led to the opening of the 50-year tradition we know as Preservation Hall, located on St. Peter Street.

An established "base" for traditional jazz attracted musicians and audiences alike, and the various incarnations of the Preservation Hall Jazz Band renewed interest in the local sound. Motivated older musicians like Danny Barker became teachers and mentors to a younger generation of teens growing up in the 1970s. Those young men had their own views on the music; some stayed with the traditional sound, while others followed a more modern path. Either way, the local jazz scene in the 1980s experienced a major boost, and jazz combos stepped up and began to compete for listeners with the R&B and funk players. Brass bands took the basics they had learned from Daniel "Danny" Barker, Ernest "Doc" Paulin, and the men of the Onward Brass Band and put their own twist on it, bringing the music out of preserved stasis. The older generations were buried in classic style, and the "walk back" was fresh and exciting.

Those who followed paths different from the traditional passed on what they knew as well. Ellis Marsalis and other "modern" players assumed the role of teacher and mentor, encouraging talented youths to stretch the boundaries. The combination of traditional and modern is too strong, even for the disaster that was Hurricane Katrina, as New Orleans jazz continues to expand and evolve in its second century.

One

BUDDY BOLDEN'S
NEW ORLEANS

Growing up in the Uptown neighborhood and riding the streetcars around town, Charles "Buddy" Bolden could not read music, so when he took up the cornet, he listened to the music of the city and made it his own. Not only did he become active in the New Orleans music scene during the early years of Storyville, from 1895 to 1906, but he also cemented a place among those of the "jazz royalty," earning the title of "King Bolden."

Turn-of-the-century New Orleans was a port city, with a diverse mixture of ethnic groups about town. Germans operated breweries, as well as restaurants and saloons where they could sell their beer directly. Italian immigrants dominated the French Quarter, so much so that this section easily could have been renamed the Italian Quarter. Meanwhile, African Americans had been free men and women for 30 years, yet still had to live apart from whites due to the Jim Crow laws, enforcing a "separate but equal" status. Despite this contradiction, it was this freedom that accounted for the major difference between the music of this period and that of earlier times in the city, as blacks were free to spend their leisure time in parks, saloons, and other places of entertainment, where they could sing songs and play instruments of their choice.

PLACE CONGO. Under French rule, city leaders allowed slaves to congregate, but in an open area just outside the original city, north of Rampart Street. This area became known as Place des Nègres, or more commonly, Place Congo. By the time Americans took control, the city had grown past the Vieux Carre, and this gathering point was called Congo Square. Bringing their drums, bells, and other musical instruments, slaves would gather in the square, roughly by tribe, to play music, sing songs, and dance. Gatherings in Congo Square continued well into the 1880s. (Courtesy of NOPL.)

OPPOSITE PAGE: **BRASH BRASS.** The emergence of brass bands in the 1890s was not universally popular. While bars and saloons in Storyville, the French Quarter, and Faubourg Ste. Marie began hiring brass bands, many property owners in those neighborhoods complained. The delicate balance between live music venues and residences is still a struggle in New Orleans neighborhoods to this day. (Courtesy of NOPL.)

Minstrel Shows. In the mid-19th century, New Orleans was one of the major entertainment capitals of North America. In 1853, it did not matter that Buckley's company did not hail from New Orleans; what did matter was that people wanted to hear music from the city. (Both, courtesy of LOC.)

RED LIGHT. In an effort to curtail prostitution in the city, New Orleans alderman Sidney Story proposed an ordinance in 1894 to create a legal red-light district in the area just north of the French Quarter, bounded by Iberville, Basin, St. Louis, and North Robertson Streets. This district, shown here in 1906, became known as Storyville, a dubious homage to its creator, and attracted brothels, nightclubs, and bars. (Courtesy of NOPL.)

STORYVILLE TODAY. The United States' entry into World War I in 1917 provided the catalyst for the closure of Storyville, as the Army did not want soldiers wandering into the district before shipping out to Europe. Little remains of the district today; it was demolished in the 1930s and replaced with a public housing project. This grocery store, photographed in 2005, had been Frank Early's Saloon a century earlier. (Courtesy of Carlos May.)

"Funky Butt." Charles "Buddy" Bolden (1877–1931) grew up in a shotgun house on First Street in Uptown New Orleans. Even though he did not read music, Bolden taught himself how to play the cornet, imitating the bands he heard in public parks and watching street parades and playing his own tunes, like the popular (and vulgar) "Funky Butt." This is the only known photograph of Bolden, taken with his band, around 1902. They are, from left to right, (front row) Jefferson Mumford and Frank Lewis; (back row) Jimmy Johnson, Bolden, Willie Cornish, and William Warner. (Above, courtesy NOPL; below, Carlos May.)

LINCOLN PARK. Located in the Riverbend section of Uptown New Orleans, Lincoln Park on South Carrollton Avenue was a popular venue for African Americans in Jim Crow New Orleans. With a roller-skating rink, dance barn, and an outdoor stage, the park regularly featured bands. Due to its location on the St. Charles streetcar line, Lincoln Park's reputation grew across the city and out into the rural areas, attracting teen musicians like Kid Ory. (Courtesy of UNO.)

BRANDING. In addition to his saloons in Storyville, Tom Anderson also owned the Arlington Café, named after Josie Arlington, who operated one of the top brothels in the district. The café offered "private dining," as discretion was important to many customers, no doubt. (Courtesy of NOPL.)

15

DUTT. Born in LaPlace, Louisiana, Edward "Dutt" Ory and his friends would take the train into New Orleans on weekends, then the streetcar to Lincoln Park, to hear Buddy Bolden and other bands. When Bolden tried to hire the teen trombonist, Ory's sister insisted he stay home with their father in LaPlace until he was 21. Dutt kept his promise and then moved into his sister's house on Jackson Avenue, pictured here. (Courtesy of Carlos May.)

TAILGATING. Bands playing at parks and dance halls on Friday and Saturday nights would regularly ride around in horse-drawn wagons in the afternoons, playing in the streets and advertising their gigs. The trombone player in this unknown 1905 band would likely follow Ory in his style—playing off the back of the wagon so the slide would not hit his fellow bandmates. (Courtesy of NOPL.)

ROLE MODEL. Antonio Junius "Tony" Jackson (1882–1921) was arguably the best piano player of the Storyville era. His incredible skill at improvisation served as a role model for many musicians playing in the district. Because Jackson had the ability to quickly copy a tune, he could then modify it and make it his own. Improvisation is one of the defining characteristics of jazz, and Jackson is considered to be one of its creators. (Courtesy of NOPL.)

STORYVILLE SALOONS. It is a common myth that jazz bands played in the brothels of Storyville. Those establishments did not welcome the loud, brash music of the likes of King Bolden or King Oliver, who played the saloons in the district instead. Lala's Big 25 was one of those saloons. Its front doors are preserved at Basin Street Station, an office building and tourist welcome center in Faubourg Treme. (Courtesy of Carlos May.)

HANGOUT. Tom Anderson was a major force and presence in Storyville. His second club was located just up Basin Street from Josie Arlington's house (in the background, with the rounded cupola). When the "sporting gentlemen" (as customers of the houses were known) finished their business at Josie's, they would stop at the saloon for a drink and to hear some music. (Courtesy of NOPL.)

COMPETITION. As King Bolden's bands grew in popularity, other band and orchestra leaders modified their style, playing the syncopated rhythms and doing more improv. One such bandleader was cornetist Freddie Keppard (1889–1933). Keppard founded the Olympia Orchestra, whose members included Alphonse Picou, Jean Vigne, Joe Petit, and Louis Keppard, Freddie's brother. (Courtesy of NPS.)

OUTSIDE STORYVILLE. While prostitution was only legal within the Storyville district, brothels and saloons popped up on the uptown side of Canal Street as well. One of the bars that regularly featured early jazz bands was the Eagle Saloon, located on the 400 block of South Rampart Street. The building has long since been repurposed as office and retail space, but it is one of the few early jazz venues still standing. (Courtesy of Carlos May.)

KID'S CANAL STREET. When Kid Ory came to New Orleans on the train from LaPlace, he would then take the Tulane Belt streetcar to Canal Street. There, he found the heart of the city's transit system and the dozens of streetcars that took New Orleanians to and from work. (Courtesy of NOPL.)

LAKEFRONT. Before the days of air-conditioning in homes, New Orleanians would take day trips to the south shore of Lake Pontchartrain to temporarily escape the summer heat. One popular lakefront destination was West End, where the New Basin Canal met the lake. (Courtesy of NOPL.)

MILITARY. While Bolden and other black bandleaders began playing syncopated rhythms, whites-only crowds still opted for Sousa-style brass band music. George DeDroit, a veteran of the Spanish-American War, organized his military-style band in 1902, playing private gigs as well as public concerts at West End. His son Johnny also led several bands in the 1910s and 1920s. (Courtesy of NOPL.)

KING. Joe "King" Oliver (1885–1938) was born in Donaldsonville, Louisiana, just north of New Orleans, and moved to the city as a boy. He played cornet extensively in the Storyville district but left New Orleans after an incident in 1919, when a fight broke out in a club and police arrested him and his band. Oliver mentored a young Louis Armstrong, who joined his band as second cornet in Chicago. Even though he never returned to New Orleans, Oliver's bands were shining examples of New Orleans Jazz throughout the 1920s. (Courtesy of SLL.)

LEGEND. Buddy Bolden's dementia grew worse in 1906. By 1907, his family had him committed to the state mental hospital in Jackson, Louisiana, where he would remain until his death in 1933. After being brought home to New Orleans, Bolden was buried in Mid-City at Holt Cemetery, a potter's field where indigent families bury their loved ones. His grave was unmarked and has been lost to time. In 1996, a group that included Bolden biographer Don Marquis (pictured) arranged to have a monument erected to Bolden in the cemetery. It was dedicated on September 6, 1996, the anniversary of Bolden's birth. (Courtesy of Carlos May.)

Two

CREOLE JAZZ

When Bolden's mental health problems incapacitated him, other bandleaders had already changed their own repertoires to include his new beats. Younger musicians like Kid Ory were ready to move up from being sidemen for Bolden, Keppard, and Oliver to leading their own bands. Jazz was more than just a fly-by-night phenomenon. The movement it created was here to stay. The desire to play music as a full-time career is a natural instinct for most musicians, so they would advertise by playing in public areas, busking for tips, which caused the music to spread from the "colored" parks and saloons to white neighborhoods and establishments. One 11-year-old, Louis "Satchmo" Armstrong, regularly made excuses to hang out around the saloons and dance halls where the bands played, and Joe Oliver took him under his wing, helping him improve his technique on the cornet. Shooting a gun off in the street landed him in juvenile detention, begging Satchmo's legendary career.

COUNTRY BAND. After spending his teen years coming into town to watch and later play music in New Orleans, Kid Ory organized his own band. In 1910, its members were, from left to right, Ed "Rabbit" Robertson, Ory, Lewis "Chif" Matthews, Johnny Brown, Joseph "Stonewall" Matthews, and Foster Lewis. (Courtesy of NOPL.)

VAUDEVILLE. Orpheum Circuit promoters put together a New Orleans band for a vaudeville tour in 1914. Though the band had rehearsed, the tour never happened. This "supergroup" included, from left to right, (first row) Ninesse Trepangier (snare drum) and Armand J. Piron (violin); (second row) Papa Celestin, Tom Benton, and Johnny St. Cyr; (third row) Clarence Williams (grandfather of the television actor Clarence Williams III), John Lindsay, Jimmie Noone, and William Ridgley. (Courtesy of NOPL.)

PROFESSIONAL. When Buddy Bolden's behavior became erratic in 1906, those who played with him began to move on to other bands. Many of those bands, such as Peter Bocage's Superior Orchestra, required their musicians be able to read music, which presented problems for those like Willie "Bunk" Johnson. Members of the Superior Orchestra in 1910 are, from left to right, (first row) Walter Brundy, drums; Peter Bocage, violin and leader; and Richard Payne, guitar; (second row) Buddy Johnson, trombone; Bunk Johnson, cornet; "Big Eye" Louis Nelson Delisle, clarinet; and Billy Marrero, string bass. (Both, courtesy of NOPL.)

BASE BALL   BASE BALL

NATIONAL BALL PARK

Washington Ave. and Claiborne

SUNDAY, JULY 4, 1915

L. R. & N. R. R. of Shreveport, La.

VS

L. R. & N. R. R. of New Orleans, La.

GAME CALLED AT 10:00 O'CLOCK A. M.

ADMISSION - - - - - 15c.

SEATS FOR COLORED

RAGTIME. Known professionally as "Jelly Roll Morton," Ferdinand Joseph LaMothe (1885–1941) was a pianist and bandleader who is now widely regarded as one of the originators of jazz. In fact, Morton was arrogant enough to claim he had invented the genre himself. As a bandleader, Morton was one of the first to actually morph jazz from merely an improvisational format into formally arranged music. He is third from left in this 1915 photograph, shot in California. (Courtesy of NOPL.)

OPPOSITE PAGE: **BASEBALL.** Baseball parks provided bands with a built-in audience that would not want leave right after an afternoon game. Occasionally, two bands would play a "cutting" session after a game, letting the audience decide which was better. National Ball Park, located uptown at Washington and Claiborne Avenues, became a regular venue for Kid Ory's band. (Courtesy of NOPL.)

TOURING. King Oliver's band is shown performing on a vaudeville tour in 1922. From left to right are Ram Hall, Honore Dutre, Oliver, Lil Armstrong, David Jones, Johnny Dodds, James A. Palao, and Montudie Garland. (Courtesy of NOPL.)

VIRTUOSO. Here, Tony Jackson accompanies three "Pretty Babies"—from left to right, Cora Green, Carolyn Williams, and Florence Mills—in 1918. Mills went on to a promising career as a singer in New York, landing a role in the 1921 musical *Shuffle Along.* Her career was cut short, however; Mills contracted tuberculosis and died in 1927. (Courtesy of NOPL.)

LOCAL. As jazz grew in popularity so did the demand for bands to play at white functions, such as this 1915 dance for Tulane University's Junior German Club. Many African American musicians refused to play whites-only parties and events, though, because they were obliged to conform with Jim Crow segregation laws by entering and exiting places via back doors and kitchens. (Courtesy of NOPL.)

Few Juveniles Arrested.

Very few arrests of minors were made Tuesday, and the bookings in the Juvenile Court are not more than the average. Six white boys were arrested in Canal street for disturbing the peace, and one for being drunk. The most serious case was that of Louis Armstrong, a twelve-year-old negro, who discharged a revolver at Rampart and Perdido streets. Being an old offender he was sent to the negro Waif's Home. The other boys were paroled.

JUVENILE. The first time Louis Armstrong's name appeared in print might have been this arrest report from January 2, 1913, published in the New Orleans *Times-Democrat* newspaper. This incident landed young Louis in the Colored Waifs' Home for Boys. (Courtesy of NOPL.)

RETURN. Armstrong (front row, center) returned to the Waifs' Home, located at 301 City Park Avenue, to pose for this 1920s photograph. There, he had received musical instruction from the home's band director, Peter Davis, from 1913 until June 1914. (Courtesy of NOPL.)

BOURBON STREET. The French Quarter was much more residential at the start of the 20th century than it is today. With the "sporting" entertainment focused on Storyville, even Rue Bourbon was a quiet neighborhood. There were some bars, such as the Absinthe House, which remains in operation today. (Courtesy of LOC.)

BOLDEN PLAYERS. The Original Creole Orchestra led by James A. Palao is shown here in 1914. From left to right are (first row) Dink Johnson, Palao, and Giggy Williams; (second row) Eddie Vinson, Freddie Keppard, George Baquet, and Bill Johnson. This band is a good example of the grouping and regrouping that regularly occurs among musicians as styles and directions change. (Courtesy of NOPL.)

FIGHTS. Baseball was not the only draw to National Baseball Park. Boxing matches also drew large crowds that were essentially captive audiences. When given the option to stick around for a dance, they did just that, dancing to jazz into the evening. (Courtesy of NOPL.)

STORYVILLE DECLINE. The Anderson Band is shown here in 1919. From left to right are Paul Barbarin, Arnold Metoyer, Luis Russell, Willie Santiago, and Albert Nicholas. Storyville's tenure as a legal red-light district ended with the United States' entry into World War I, but the saloons continued to offer entertainment. (Courtesy of NOPL.)

BLUES BAND. When Buddy Bolden left the scene, Frank Dusen took over his group, renaming it the Eagle Band, after the Eagle Saloon on South Rampart Street. By 1919, the band consisted of, from left to right, (seated) Warren Dodds and Bunk Johnson; (standing) Johnny Dodds, Dusen, Peter Bocage, and Bill Johnson. (Courtesy of LSM.)

Red Book. Here is an advertisement for Miss Josie Arlington's Sporting Palace, located at 225 Basin Street. Arlington was one of the most successful of the Storyville madams. Contrary to the various tales and legends of Storyville, establishments like Arlington's did not hire jazz bands. At most, they would have a single piano for background music. (Courtesy of NOPL.)

MISS
JOSIE ARLINGTON

225 Basin Street   Phone 1888

Nowhere in this country will you find a more complete and thorough sporting establishment than the Arlington.

Absolutely and unquestionably the most decorative and costly fitted out sporting palace ever placed before the American public.

The wonderful originality of everything that goes to fit out a mansion makes it the most attractive ever seen in this and the old country.

Miss Arlington recently went to an expense of nearly $5,000 in having her mansion renovated and replenished.

Within the great walls of the Arlington will be found the work of great artists from Europe and America. Many articles from the Louisiana Purchase Exposition will also be seen.

The Arlington

Up the Line. Arlington's establishment was not the only high-class place on Basin Street, as seen in this 1910 real-photo postcard. The US Army demanded that the city close its brothels once they began to use New Orleans as a port of embarkation for Europe. (Courtesy of NOPL.)

OLYMPIA. From left to right, Joe, Ricard, and Peter Alexis, three members of Freddie Keppard's Olympia Orchestra, are shown here in 1915. This was the original incarnation of Olympia; in 1958, Harold Dejan split from the Eureka Brass Band, reviving the name Olympia. Dejan's band continues to play today. (Courtesy of LSM.)

SPANISH FORT. The area near the ruins of Fort St. John, known as the "Old Spanish Fort" that guarded access to the city from Lake Pontchartrain, was a popular entertainment center at the turn of the 19th century. Over the Rhine was one of the nightclubs that regularly engaged bands. (Courtesy of NOPL.)

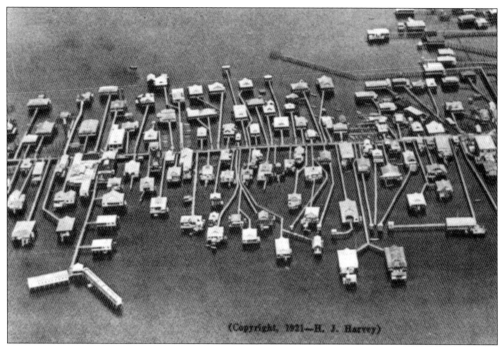

(Copyright, 1921—H. J. Harvey.)

"SMOKY MARY." Located in what is now the Gentilly neighborhood, Milneburg was a popular lakefront area for fishing camps and summer homes. Bands such as Kid Ory's would take the steam train, the "Smoky Mary," to Milneburg, then go door-to-door playing for tips. (Courtesy of NOPL.)

EAST END. To the west of the New Basin Canal was Jefferson Parish. Originally a fishing village, Bucktown was the neighborhood along the parish line with the city. Saloons and gambling parlors opened in this area, and naturally, the jazz bands followed. (Courtesy of NOPL.)

PRESERVATION. So few original buildings associated with the early jazz period remain in downtown New Orleans. The Iroquois Theater, located on South Rampart Street near Perdido Street, is part of the struggle to preserve this precious heritage. (Courtesy of Carlos May.)

"EVERY SUNDAY."

LINCOLN PARK,

SUNDAY, APRIL 22.

FREE

Open Air Concert
—BY—
Excelsior Brass Band.

BALLOON ASCENSION
—AND—
PARACHUTE LEAP
By Prof. L. B. Haddock,
of Boston.

5 p. m.

In the Auditorium, 8 P. M.
High Class Vaudeville and Novelty Act.
Dance.......er Programme.
Take St. Charles Belt and Tulane Cars.

EXCELSIOR. Even as jazz took hold downtown and in Storyville, the music was just as strong uptown. Live shows featuring balloons and parachute drops were popular draws to Lincoln Park. On this particular evening, the Excelsior Band provided entertainment to close out the night. (Courtesy of UNO.)

KING ON THE ROAD. In 1918, Los Angeles bassist Kid Ory found himself with a gig in Chicago and no band with which to play it. He contacted King Oliver, who came up from New Orleans, along with Paul Barbarin and Jimmie Noone. By 1921, Oliver took control, and the band became known as King Oliver's Creole Jazz Band. They played together for two years but, unfortunately, did not record. Band members are, from left to right, Honore Dutrey, Baby Dodds, King Oliver, Lil Hardin, Bill Johnson, and Johnny Dodds; Louis Armstrong is kneeling in front, playing a slide trumpet. (Courtesy of NOPL.)

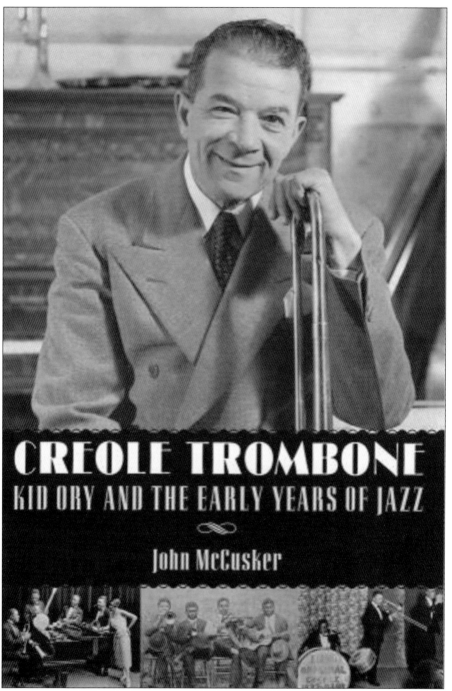

CONTINUITY. Kid Ory bookends the Creole period of jazz in New Orleans, because he played a significant role in carrying New Orleans jazz from Lincoln Park to the rest of the world. John McCusker's 2012 book on Ory is a definitive and colorful survey of the jazz experience in turn-of-the-century New Orleans. Like many Creoles musicians, Ory took his music away from the segregated South, firmly establishing New Orleans as the birthplace of jazz. (Courtesy of John McCusker.)

Three

DIXIELAND GOES NATIONWIDE

Starting in the mid-1910s, African Americans from the mostly rural, former Confederate states began leaving their homes in large numbers. They headed north to the industrial cities and west to California. The motivations for this Great Migration were almost as varied as the people who moved, but two themes were common: the search for better jobs and the desire to leave the segregated life of the South. When New Orleanians left for the North and West, they took jazz with them. Like Bolden sitting in Johnson Park, Ory, Keppard, Oliver, and others played in their new homes and drew musicians to them. Once established, they sent for other players from home. Jazz spread like wildfire in the early 1920s.

The late 1910s and early 1920s also mark the point when white musicians began to take jazz seriously, and the beats ceased to be just a "black thing." Nick Larocca wrote "Tiger Rag" in 1917, and the Original Dixieland Jass Band (ODJB) began to play it. They quickly changed the spelling of the band's name to "Jazz" when it was clear that the music was neither separate nor equal, but universal.

CAMPUS PLAYERS. By the 1920s, white musicians took up the beats of the Creole bands in numbers, as evidenced by the Tulanians, a group of students from Tulane University. The group (unidentified in this photograph) is shown playing a football-season school function. (Courtesy of NOPL.)

NORK. New Orleans–style jazz was firmly entrenched in Chicago by the 1920s. The New Orleans Rhythm Kings is an example of the combination of musicians from the two cities. Its members are, from left to right, George Brunies, trombone (New Orleans); bandleader Paul Mares, trumpet (New Orleans); Leon Roppolo, saxophone (New Orleans); Mel Sitzel, piano (Chicago); Volly De Faut, saxophone (Chicago); Lew Black, banjo (Chicago); and Steve Brown, sousaphone and bass (New Orleans). In the back is Ben Pollack, drums (Chicago). (Courtesy of LSM.)

ROLLIN'. Steamboats were used for both commerce and entertainment in the 1920s. Captains making the run from New Orleans to St. Louis and back would often engage a band for the cruise for passenger entertainment, offering musicians a chance at steady employment. Pictured here are the *Belle of Calhoun* (left) and the *Belle of the Bends*. (Courtesy of LOC.)

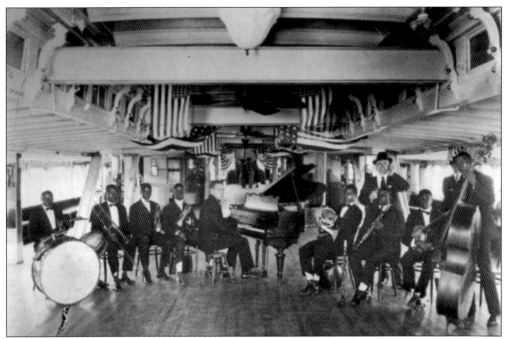

RIVER RUN. Fate Marable landed a gig aboard the SS *Sidney*, a Streckfus Lines excursion boat, and went about organizing bands for the line. This band included, from left to right, Warren "Baby" Dodds, drums; William "Bebé" Ridgley, trombone; Joe Howard, cornet; Louis Armstrong, cornet; Fate Marable, piano; David Jones, French horn; Johnny Dodds, clarinet; Johnny St. Cyr, banjo; and George "Pops" Foster, string bass. The white man (in hat) standing behind Johnny Dodds may be John Streckfus, the boat's owner. (Courtesy of NOPL.)

CAPITOL. Another Marable band is pictured here, this time from the SS *Capitol*. From left to right are Henry Kimball, bass; Boyd Atkins, violin; Johnny St. Cyr, banjo; David Jones, saxophone; Norman Mason, saxophone; Louis Armstrong, cornet; George Brashear, trombone; and Warren "Baby" Dodds, drums. Above the group is bandleader Fate Marable, on piano. (Courtesy of NOPL.)

CALIFORNIA. Papa Mutt Carey led the Jeffersonians in Los Angeles in 1924. The band included, from left to right, Leo Davis, Bud Scott, Ram Hall, Carey, and L.S. Cooper. (Courtesy of LSM.)

KID. Edward "Kid" Ory is shown in Los Angeles in 1924. Ory and his wife, Elizabeth, left New Orleans in 1919 during part of what became known in the United States as the Great Migration. In New Orleans music circles, the exodus was known as the New Orleans Music Diaspora. (Courtesy of LSM.)

KING'S DRUMS. Warren "Baby" Dodds (1898–1959), the younger brother of clarinetist Johnny Dodds, was one of the top drummers of the pre–big band era. After having disagreements about style with Fate Marable, Dodds and Louis Armstrong left Marable's band, joining Dodds's older brother in King Oliver's band. (Courtesy of NOPL.)

CHICAGO. Drummer Francis Mosely (left) led Francois and His Louisianians, which included Kid Punch Miller (center) and Charles Ducasting (right). Originally from Raceland, Louisiana, Miller also played with Jelly Roll Morton in Chicago, eventually returning to New Orleans in his later years to play at Preservation Hall. (Courtesy of NOPL.)

CONVERSION. In 1919, the influence of Tom Brown (trombone) and Tony Giardina (clarinet) turned Clint Bush's Band into a jazz combo. Bush is seen on the right (banjo). In the mid-1920s, Brown returned home to New Orleans, where he played with Johnny Bayersdorffer and recorded. (Courtesy of LSM.)

WELCOME. All-time great vaudeville comic Joe Frisco greets the Tom Brown Band from Dixieland upon their arrival in Chicago in the 1920s. Brown is directly behind Frisco, wearing a straw hat and playing the trombone. To the right of Brown are, from left to right, Ray Lopez, Larry Shields, and Deacon Loyacano. (Courtesy of NOPL.)

YACHTING. Wealthy New Orleanians occasionally engaged bands to play parties on their yachts. The 6 & 7/8's String Band played on Adm. Ernest Jahncke's yacht, the *Aunt Dinah*, in 1921. They are, from left to right, (first row) Howard McCaleb, Charles Hardy, Hilton "Midget" Harrison, Edmond Souchon, and Bill Gibbons; (second row) Bob Reynolds, Admiral Jahncke, and Shields O'Reardon. (Courtesy of NOPL.)

OKEH RECORDS. This is the first incarnation of Louis Armstrong's Hot Five. They are, from left to right, Armstrong, Johnny St. Cyr, Johnny Dodds, Kid Ory, and Lil Hardin Armstrong. This was the first band "Pops" took into the recording studio, in 1927–1928. Armstrong used musicians he played with in New Orleans. (Courtesy of NOPL.)

ORIGINAL DIXIELAND. Johnny Stein's Original Dixieland Jass Band is shown here in 1916. They are, from left to right, Alcide Nunez, Edwin Edwards, Henry Ragas, James Larocca, and leader Johnny Stein. The band would change the spelling of its name from "Jass" to "Jazz" in 1917. (Courtesy of LSM.)

NOLA TO NYC. As seen here, the Original Dixieland Jazz Band featured, from left to right, pianist Henry Ragas, clarinetist Larry Shields, trombonist Edwin Edwards, cornetist Dominick James LaRocca, and drummer Tony Sbarbaro. The band would later record the first jazz single, "Livery Stable Blues." (Courtesy of NOPL.)

BOURBON STREET. The Jules Bauduc Orchestra is shown here in 1928 playing at the Silver Slipper, located at 426 Bourbon Street. They are, from left to right, Mike Lala, Luther Lamar, Roland Leach, Monk Hazel, Paul Peque, Jules Bauduc, Horace Diaz, Eddie Powers, and Oscar Marcour. (Courtesy of NOPL.)

ON THE WATER. For a party in 1923, Admiral Jahncke hired members of both the Tuxedo Orchestra and the Young Tuxedo Orchestra. Members of the combined band are, from left to right, (seated) Henry Julian, Bush Hall, Willard Thoumy, Lawrence Marrero, and John Marrero; (standing) Chinee Forster, Milford Dolliole, Bebé Ridgley, Bob Thomas, Duck Ernest Johnson, and Eddie Marrero. (Courtesy of NOPL.)

PUBLICITY PHOTOGRAPH. Members of the Emmanuel Perez Orchestra are seen here posing for the camera. They are, from left to right, (seated) Alfred Williams, drums; Earl Humphrey, trombone; Eddie Cherie, baritone sax; Adolphe Alexander Jr., alto sax; and Caffrey Darensburg, banjo; (standing) Osceola Blanchard, piano; Emmanuel Perez, trumpet; and two unidentified. (Courtesy of LSM.)

COTTON CLUB. Armond Piron's band traveled to New York in 1923 to play the Cotton Club. Unlike many other African American musicians, these musicians did not join the diaspora, choosing instead to play in New Orleans. The band, led by violinist Piron (standing, right), consisted of, from left to right, Peter Bocage, trumpet; Bob Ysaguirre, trombone; Louis Cottrell, drums; Louis Warnacke, alto sax; Lorenzo Tio, clarinet and tenor sax; Steve Louis, piano; and Charles Bocage, banjo. (Courtesy of NOPL.)

Season's Greetings and All Good Wishes

CHRISTMAS. King Oliver sent out this holiday card in the early 1920s. Oliver's band at the time included, from left to right, (seated) Baby Dodds, Honore Dutrey, Louis Armstrong, Johnny Dodds, and Lil Hardin Armstrong; (standing) Oliver and Bill Johnson. (Courtesy of NOPL.)

SAZERAC BALLROOM. Even though the best of the Creole players went off to other parts of the country, jazz continued to grow back home. Here are members of the Original New Orleans Owls in 1924. They are, from left to right, Dick Mackie, cornet; Monk Smith, saxophone; Red Mackie, bass (standing); Benjy White, saxophone; Eblen Rau, violin (standing); Rene Gelpi, banjo; and Earl Crumb, drums and bandleader. (Courtesy of NOPL.)

EARLY LOUIS. Louis Prima's first band is shown here in 1922. The members are, from left to right, Prima, Ewell Lamar, unidentified, Irving Fazola, Johnny Viviano, and unidentified. The man in the black jacket (presumably the bandleader) is also unidentified. (Courtesy of NOPL.)

WEST END LINE. Situated halfway between downtown and West End, the appropriately named Halfway House was a nightclub located where the West End streetcar line turned off Canal Street and onto City Park Avenue. In 1923, the house orchestra consisted of, from left to right, Charlie Cordilla, Mickey Marcour, Leon Roppolo, Abbie Brunies, Bill Eastwood, Joe Loyacano, and Leo Adde. (Courtesy of LSM.)

YOUNG MUSICIANS. A group of teens practice with a mentor in front of a brewery on Jackson Avenue in 1912. Many of these youths would become well known throughout the city in only a decade. Those holding instruments are, from left to right, Happy Schilling, George Brunies, Abbie Brunies, Harry Shannon, Richie Brunies, and Bud Loyacano. (Courtesy of NOPL.)

BY THE LAKE. The Lakefront Loungers—from left to right, Abbie Brunies, Charlie Cordilla, and Stalebread Lacoume—are pictured here in West End in 1920. West End was a somewhat rural area until the 1940s, so it was easy for young musicians to hang out and practice music. They would play in West End Park for tips or find gigs at the hotels and nightclubs. (Courtesy of NOPL.)

0417 VIEW OF GROTTOS AND CAVERNS. THE CAVE - GRUNEWALD HOTEL, NEW ORLEANS, LA.

CANAL STREET JAZZ. As jazz became more popular in the New Orleans white community, large hotels picked up on the trend as well. The Grunewald Hotel on Canal Street (now the Roosevelt Hotel) operated The Cave, a nightclub on the first floor, from 1918 to 1927. The club's theme was a literal interpretation, with stalactites hanging from the ceiling. (Courtesy of NOPL.)

SENSATION. Edwin B. ("Eddie" or "Daddy") Edwards (1891–1963) played both violin and trombone with "Papa" Jack Laine in the early days. Alcide Nunez asked Edwards to go to Chicago with him to join Stein's band. Edwards was the trombonist for the ODJB until he was drafted to serve in the Army during World War I. Upon his return to the United States, he formed a couple of bands in Chicago. He rejoined the ODJB in 1936, when James "Nick" Larocca reformed the group. Benny Goodman performed his piece "Sensation" at Carnegie Hall in 1938. (Courtesy of NOPL.)

RHYTHM KING. Paul Mares was a trumpeter and leader of the New Orleans Rhythm Kings (NORK). He left New Orleans for Chicago in 1919, when Abbie Brunies declined the NORK gig. Mares returned to New Orleans in 1924 to take over his family's business from his father, who was also a cornet/trumpet player. Mares continued to play part-time in town, holding jam sessions at his home in Faubourg St. John (below). Those jam sessions became legendary when he purchased a larger house in Metairie and invited both local and Chicago musicians to join him. (At left, courtesy of LSM; below, Carlos May.)

PARIS. A very sullen-looking Sidney Bechet (right) joins New Orleanian Henry Saparo (holding banjo) in Benny Payton's Orchestra in Paris in the early 1920s. Touring in Europe was a hard life for American musicians at the time since they were all but totally cut off from home. (Courtesy of NOPL.)

WIGGS. John Wigginton Hyman (1899–1977) began his musical career as a violinist before switching to the cornet and trumpet. In the late 1920s, he took a job in New Orleans as a teacher at the State Band and Orchestra School, playing gigs at night with his band, John Hyman's Bayou Stompers. Under the name Johnny Wiggs, he played music full-time in the 1940s. (Courtesy of LSM.)

SOULFUL. Johnny Dodds (1892–1940) played clarinet and alto sax in Kid Ory's band in the 1910s, as well as on the riverboats with Fate Marable. He left New Orleans to join King Oliver's band in 1921, playing with Oliver until his band broke up in 1924. He then replaced Alcide Nunez as the clarinetist in the house band at Kelly's Stables in addition to recording with Louis Armstrong. Though a musician first, Dodds also was part owner of a Chicago taxicab company with his brothers. (Courtesy of LSM.)

INFLUENTIAL. Because so few of the early jazz greats were recorded while they were in New Orleans, the 1927 recordings of Sam Morgan's band are highly regarded. Morgan's band included, from left to right, (seated) Nolan Williams, Isaiah Morgan, Sam Morgan, Earl Fouche, Andrew Morgan, and Johnny Dave; (standing) Jim Robinson and Sidney Brown. (Courtesy of NOPL.)

YELLOW. Born in St. Bernard Parish, Alcide Nunez (1884–1934) was of Isleño heritage, which led to his nickname "Yellow." Nunez grew up in Faubourg Marigny, where he learned clarinet and became a regular in "Papa" Jack Laine's band. He left New Orleans for Chicago in 1916, playing with Stein's Dixie Jass Band, then the ODJB, but resigned from the band before they recorded. He also played with Tom Brown and spent some time playing in New York City. (Courtesy of NOPL.)

MISSED OPPORTUNITY. Frank Christian (1887–1973) was the first choice of Alcide Nunez, Eddie Edwards, and Johnny Stein to be the trumpet player in Stein's band in Chicago. Christian declined, however, since he and his New Orleans band had a full schedule, figuring it was safer for him to stay at home. Christian (right), shown here in a promotional photograph with Alcide Nunez (left) and Tom Brown, later went north, first to Chicago, then to New York City. There, he formed the Original New Orleans Jazz Band, with Jimmie Durante on the piano. When that band broke up, he toured throughout the 1920s, playing vaudeville and various gigs. (Courtesy of LSM.)

PRESERVATION FAILURE. The Halfway House is seen here in its prime as a jazz club (above) and in its death throes (below). After remaining vacant for a time, the building, located on City Park Avenue near the beginning of Canal Street, became the office of a pest-control company. When that company vacated, preservationists made efforts to restore it, but a fire in 2002, combined with damage from Hurricane Katrina in 2005, made that endeavor impossible. It was demolished in 2008. (Above, courtesy of NOPL; below, Carlos May.)

Four

DIXIELAND DECLINE

The Great Depression made it difficult for many musicians to make a living. Journeymen players were forced to give up their passion professionally, taking on other jobs merely to survive. In some cases, the country's economic collapse destroyed even the top-tier musicians. King Oliver, for example, lost all his savings when the Chicago bank he used collapsed, and he died in poverty. Many of the stars survived, however, such as Ory in Los Angeles and Armstrong in New York, along with Larocca and Bonano, who floated back and forth between Chicago, New York, and New Orleans. The music itself also evolved and changed as radio grew in popularity and the big-band sound came on the scene. It was harder for small clubs and saloons to stay afloat, so musicians migrated to larger orchestras. By the 1950s, when historians and true fans of the genre realized the original generation of jazz musicians was growing old and dying, heightened efforts were launched to record their music and preserve their stories.

ON THE RADIO. WSMB Radio's house orchestra is pictured here in 1930. The station's offices and studios were located on the 13th floor of the Maison Blanche Building, at the intersection of Canal and Dauphine Streets downtown. The members are, from left to right, Mr. Gorman, cello; Albert Fisher, bass; Carl Mandever, violin; Mr. Pertuit, piano; Bill Gillen, trumpet; Pascal Ugarte, drums; Irving Fazola, sax/clarinet; Sal Finnegella Sr., trumpet; Sal Finnegella Jr., sax/clarinet; and Charlie Kigsky, trombone. The two men on the far right are unidentified. (Courtesy of LSM.)

RCA SESSION. This is Jelly Roll Morton's last recording session, in 1939, for RCA. Pictured from left to right are (front) Sidney Bechet on clarinet, Albert Nicholas on clarinet, and Albert "Happy" Cauldwell on saxophone; (back) Sidney DeParis on trumpet, Zutty Singleton on drums, and Jelly Roll Morton on piano. Morton passed away two years later. (Courtesy of LSM.)

ZUTTY. Arthur "Zutty" Singleton (1898–1975) started like many New Orleans musicians in the early 1900s by playing pickup gigs and theater lobbies. He served (and was wounded) in the US Navy during World War I. Upon his return to New Orleans, he played with a number of jazz bands, including those of Papa Celestin, Big Eye Louis Nelson, and John Robichaux, as well as on riverboats with Fate Marable. In the 1920s, Singleton moved to Chicago and, in 1928, replaced Baby Dodds on the drums for the second incarnation of Louis Armstrong's Hot Five. He then followed Armstrong to New York in 1929. Seen here around 1939, Singleton (drums) is with Joe Marsala (clarinet) and Teddy Wilson (piano) at the National Press Club in Washington, DC. (Courtesy of LOC.)

GIGOLO. Louis Prima (1910–1978) was from a Sicilian family who lived in New Orleans. Prima played trumpet in a number of Italian-owned clubs in town, but his vocals garnered him much more recognition. Moving to New York in 1934, he organized the New Orleans Gang, combining scat and swing with traditional Dixieland. Prima moved out to Los Angeles, mainly to avoid entanglements with the Italian mob. He opened the Famous Door nightclub, which led to movie appearances. In 1937, Prima returned to New York, where he began to record and perform Italian songs such as "Angelina." After meeting Keely Smith in 1951, the two began to record together and were married a short time thereafter, later divorcing in 1961. Prima was chosen for the voice of King Louie in Disney's *The Jungle Book* in 1967. (Courtesy of LOC.)

BANJO. Johnny St. Cyr (1890–1966) played in the Olympia, Superior, and Tuxedo Orchestras and then on riverboats with Fate Marable during the 1910s. He went to Chicago with King Oliver and later became a member of Louis Armstrong's Hot Five. He is seen here recording with the Original Creole Stompers in 1949. Pictured from left to right are Louis Nelson, trombone; Herb Morand, trumpet; Austin Young, bass; Albert Burbank, clarinet; and Johnny St. Cyr, guitar. Albert Jiles is on drums, partially visible on the left. (Courtesy of LSM.)

DISNEY. Here, Kid Ory plays on a riverboat at Disneyland as part of the Young Men of New Orleans in 1960. Johnny St. Cyr (barely visible on left, behind Ory) led the group from 1960 until his death in 1966. (Courtesy of LSM.)

SECOND LINE. The tradition of the second-line parade is a long one. This Stanley Kubrick photograph from 1950 shows the Eureka Brass Band as the "first line" in a parade of the Signs of the Zodiac Social Aid and Pleasure Club, which is the "second line" to the band. The sax player is unidentified; the sousaphone player is Joseph "Red" Clark. (Courtesy of LOC.)

DUKES. The original Dukes of Dixieland was a family band, formed by the Assuntos in 1948, with brothers Frank and Fred on the trumpet and trombone, respectively, and their father, "Papa Jac," on the trombone and banjo. They recorded regularly and played around town. This photograph shows the band playing at the Municipal Auditorium in 1950. From left to right are Frank Assunto, trombone; Monk Hazel, drums; Fred Assunto, trumpet; Chink Martin, bass (behind Fred Assunto); Jeff Riddick, piano; and Pete Fountain, clarinet. Sharkey Bonano is on the right. (Courtesy of LSM.)

BANANA. Joseph "Sharkey" Bonano (1904–1972) was born in the Milneburg neighborhood of New Orleans. As a youth, he played locally before he began to travel. In the late 1920s and early 1930s, he played with the Original Dixieland Jazz Band, replacing Nick Larocca. Unlike many New Orleans musicians, "Sharkey Banana" (at the mic) often returned to New Orleans to record and play, as seen here with his band in 1950. (Courtesy of LOC.)

EDUCATION. During the Great Depression, government programs like the Works Progress Administration (WPA) sponsored education programs for teens. Musicians and teachers were trained to work with young people, and then they went out to teach music. (Courtesy of NOPL.)

DANCING. At left is a 1940s advertisement for the Dew Drop nightclub, hotel, and barbershop, located on LaSalle Street in New Orleans. From the 1930s to the mid-1960s, the Dew Drop was a popular dance venue, attracting a number of jazz groups as well as emerging R&B and rock-n-roll performers. Below, the club's sign is shown how it appears today. (At left, courtesy of NOPL; below, Carlos May.)

JUMBO. Grammy-winning trumpet player Al Hirt (1922–1999) was a man of many talents. In addition to recording the theme song for the 1960s superhero show *The Green Hornet*, Hirt was the owner of a Bourbon Street nightclub and a minority owner of the New Orleans Saints when the team was created in 1967. Widely regarded as an ambassador of New Orleans, Hirt also was one of the founders of the Krewe of Bacchus carnival parade. (At right, courtesy of NNA; below, LSM.)

BLUE ROOM, THE ROOSEVELT, NEW ORLEANS, LOUISIANA

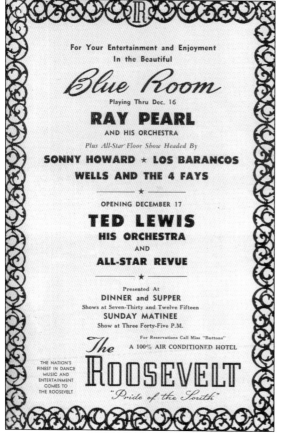

For Your Entertainment and Enjoyment
In the Beautiful

Blue Room

Playing Thru Dec. 16

RAY PEARL

AND HIS ORCHESTRA

Plus All-Star Floor Show Headed By

SONNY HOWARD ★ LOS BARANCOS

WELLS AND THE 4 FAYS

— ★ —

OPENING DECEMBER 17

TED LEWIS

HIS ORCHESTRA

AND

ALL-STAR REVUE

— ★ —

Presented At

DINNER and SUPPER

Shows at Seven-Thirty and Twelve Fifteen

SUNDAY MATINEE

Show at Three Forty-Five P.M.

For Reservations Call Miss "Buttons"

A 100% AIR CONDITIONED HOTEL

THE NATION'S
FINEST IN DANCE
MUSIC AND
ENTERTAINMENT
COMES TO
THE ROOSEVELT

The

ROOSEVELT

"Pride of the South"

BIG BANDS. New Orleans hotels, such as the Roosevelt on Canal Street, embraced the swing era of the big bands in the 1930s and 1940s. The Roosevelt's Blue Room featured a big band as its house orchestra. Unfortunately, the drain on local talent that hit New Orleans in the 1930s to 1940s meant that hotels had to book non-native dance orchestras. Ray Pearl's orchestra would periodically come down from Chicago to play the Blue Room. Though originally from Ohio, Ted Lewis began to copy New Orleans–style jazz in the 1910s. By the 1930s, he was leading a swing-style big band. The Roosevelt continues to offer musical entertainment in the Blue Room as well as the Fountain Lounge. (Both, courtesy of NOPL.)

REVIVAL CATALYST. William Gary "Bunk" Johnson (1879–1949) claimed to be a member of Buddy Bolden's band, but research into the early years indicates he was not a regular. Johnson (left) lost his front teeth in a fight in 1931, but was able to get dentures by 1939. He made his first recordings in 1942 and enjoyed some success while touring in the mid-1940s, such as this gig in New York City, where he played with Lead Belly. (Courtesy of NOPL.)

REVIVAL LEADER. Born Joseph Louis Francois Zenon in the French Quarter, George Lewis (1900–1968) began his professional career in 1917, playing for Buddy Petit, Kid Ory, and Chris Kelly. Unlike many other talented black musicians, Lewis did not leave New Orleans. He worked for several years as a stevedore during the Great Depression, moonlighting with several bands. Lewis became better known in the 1940s, when Bunk Johnson chose him to play clarinet in his revival band. When Johnson's health declined, Lewis took over leadership of the band, playing with Lewis Marrero, Al Pavageau, Jim Robinson, Alton Purnell, and Baby Dodds. By the 1960s, Lewis was playing regularly at Preservation Hall, influencing a new generation of players. (Courtesy of NOPL.)

YOUNG EAGLE. Leeds "Lee" Collins (1901–1960) played with the Young Eagles, the Columbia Band, and the Tuxedo Brass Band as a teenager. He later replaced Louis Armstrong on cornet in King Oliver's band in Chicago and also played with Jelly Roll Morton. In Chicago, in the 1930s and 1940s, Collins (center) played with the Dodds brothers, Zutty Singleton, and several other New Orleans musicians. Returning to New Orleans, Collins helped form the Jones-Collins Astoria Hot Eight, named after the Astoria Hotel on Rampart Street. After 1945, he led the house band at the Victory Club, where this photograph was taken on his 50th birthday. (Courtesy of NOPL.)

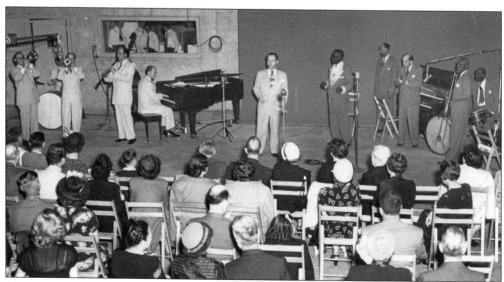

BATTLE OF THE BANDS. Recorded at the French Quarter studios of WDSU in 1950, Sharkey Bonano's band played with/against Papa Celestin's band. Bonano's band consisted of Sharkey, Lester Bouchon, Charlie Miller, Jeff Riddick, Chink Martin Sr., and Monk Hazel. Papa's band included Celestin, Alphonse Picou, Bill Matthews, and Louis Barbarin. (Courtesy of LSM.)

Pops. Louis "Pops" Armstrong (1901–1971) went from the streets of New Orleans and the Colored Waifs' Home for Boys to playing for King Oliver and following him to Chicago. Armstrong spent most of the Great Depression in California. He achieved commercial success in both Chicago and New York, hitting his peak when "Hello Dolly" knocked The Beatles off the top of the pop charts. While he never returned to New Orleans for more than a few visits, Armstrong is considered the main icon of New Orleans jazz. (Above, courtesy of LOC; at right, LSM.)

HISTORIAN. Edmond "Doc" Souchon (1897–1968) was one of the early leaders in the historical preservation of New Orleans jazz. While studying to become a physician in Chicago, Souchon played with a number of bands in the 1910s. He later recorded in the 1940s and was at the forefront of the establishment of the New Orleans Jazz Club and the New Orleans Jazz Museum. (Courtesy of LSM.)

MINT CONDITION. Doc Souchon's efforts to preserve the jazz heritage of New Orleans came to fruition with the establishment of the New Orleans Jazz Club in 1949, which led to the opening of the New Orleans Jazz Museum in 1961. The museum had several locations over time, including the Royal Sonesta on Bourbon Street, and accumulated an interesting collection of memorabilia, such as Eddie Edwards's trombone. (Edwards is shown here donating the instrument to Souchon and the museum.) The museum went bankrupt in 1973, and the collection went into storage. It was subsequently donated to the Louisiana State Museum, which reopened the collection in 1978 at the Old US Mint on Esplanade Avenue. (Courtesy of LSM.)

Five

Brass Bands and Traditional Jazz

Larry Borenstein's desire to work and hear music truly became something magical when older musicians started coming by his art gallery in the French Quarter to play. When the concept turned into something serious by 1960, the music had a home where it could be heard any night of the week. Preservation Hall's success guaranteed that "traditional" jazz (the term now used since "Dixieland" is regarded by many to have segregationist overtones) would live on.

Writers of the *New York Times* and other national papers remarked about the infrequency with which New Orleans–style brass band music was heard, primarily only at "jazz funerals." Thus, musicians like Danny Barker stepped up and began to teach a new generation of horn players and drummers how to play and march in parades. Soon, brass bands were popping up once again as if it were the late 1910s. That trend is still going strong. Like Buddy Bolden, the younger musicians take the traditional and make it their own, adding hip-hop, electronics, and other sounds.

ONWARD. Adolphe Paul Barbarin (1899–1969), seen here performing for the New Orleans Jazz Club in 1964, played with Oliver and Armstrong in Chicago and New York. He returned to New Orleans in 1960 to found, with Louis Cottrell Jr., a second incarnation of the Onward Brass Band. Barbarin composed a number of Dixieland tunes, including "Bourbon Street Parade." (Courtesy of LSM.)

ACTIVIST. It is only natural that, with Manny Perez as his godfather, Louis Cottrell Jr. (1911–1978) grew up around many of the New Orleans early jazz greats. Cottrell (left) played with "Polo" Barnes, Chris Kelly, and others in the 1920s, as well as on riverboats with the Young Tuxedo Brass Band. In the 1930s, Cottrell became a union organizer, encouraging African American musicians to join the Colored Musicians Union and to have that union recognized as a local in the American Federation of Musicians. He is seen here playing with Joe Thomas. (Courtesy of LSM.)

BRASS REVIVAL. The original Onward Brass Band played from 1886 to 1930. Paul Barbarin and Louis Cottrell Jr. formed a new incarnation of Onward in 1960. Seen here, they are, from left to right, (kneeling) Alvin Alcorn on trumpet, Cag Cagnolatti on trumpet, Paul Barbarin on drums, and two unidentified; (standing) Kid Howard on trumpet, Louis Cottrell Jr. on clarinet, Louis Barbarin on drums, and three unidentified. (Courtesy of LSM.)

LEGACY. The grandson of Isidore Barbarin and the nephew of drummers Paul and Louis Barbarin, Daniel Moses "Danny" Barker (1909–1994) originally played clarinet and drums before switching to banjo. In New York in the 1930s, Barker played with a number of jazz greats and was a sideman in the studio for Cab Calloway. He returned to New Orleans in 1965, played with the Onward Brass Band, and became an assistant curator at the New Orleans Jazz Museum. In 1970, he founded the legendary Fairview Baptist Church Marching Band, which launched the careers of many of today's New Orleans jazz musicians. (Courtesy of Carlos May.)

INCUBATOR. In 1970, Danny Barker organized a youth band based out of the Fairview Baptist Church in New Orleans. The band produced many notable alumni, including Wynton and Branford Marsalis, Dr. Michael White, Anthony "Tuba Fats" Lacen, Kirk Joseph, and Shannon Powell. (Courtesy of NOPL.)

YOUTH. Seen here in the early 1970s are members of the Fairview Baptist Church Marching Band, including Dr. Michael White on clarinet. The band was not without controversy, however, as some union musicians claimed that Barker's use of non-union youths was exploitive. He disbanded the group in 1974, but Leroy Jones immediately reformed it as the Hurricane Brass Band, which eventually became the Dirty Dozen Brass Band. (Courtesy of LSM.)

TRADITIONAL. In the 1950s, art gallery proprietor and jazz aficionado Larry Borenstein began inviting many of the living jazz legends in the city to rehearse at his place, located at 732 St. Peter Street in the French Quarter. Allan and Sandra Jaffe discovered Associated Artists in 1960, by which time the jam sessions in the gallery had become nightly events. The following year, Borenstein moved the art gallery next door and turned over the music operations to the Jaffes, marking the birth of Preservation Hall. Now operated by a nonprofit foundation, Preservation Hall features nightly band performances from 8:00 p.m. to 11:00 p.m. Famed New Orleans night spot Pat O'Briens is visible just down the block. (Courtesy of Carlos May.)

MAINSTAY. Louis Hall Nelson (1902–1990) began his career on the trombone at the age of 15. He played with many of the New Orleans greats in the 1920s and then joined a WPA band during the Depression. Enlisting in the US Navy during World War II, Nelson played in a Navy band in Memphis, earning the rank of musician, first class. Upon returning to New Orleans, Nelson played with Sidney Desvigne's Orchestra before joining the Kid Thomas Valentine Band. In 1961, he became a regular in the fledgling Preservation Hall venue, which exposed him to a new and younger audience. Offers to play and tour came in, and Nelson did just that, right up to his tragic death, the result of a hit-and-run automobile accident. (Courtesy of NOPL.)

TUXEDO REVIVAL. Gregg Stafford (standing) took over leadership of the Young Tuxedo Brass Band in 1984. He is seen here, along with fellow Fairview alumnus Dr. Michael White (left foreground, holding clarinet) and the rest of the band, performing at the New Orleans Jazz & Heritage Festival in 2010. (Courtesy of Carlos May.)

DOZEN. When the Fairview Baptist Band disbanded, 12 of its members formed the Dirty Dozen Brass Band in 1977. The band's mix of traditional jazz with R&B and other forms of jazz gave them a unique sound and an incredible amount of popularity and commercial success. Fairview alumnus and original Dirty Dozen member Roger Lewis plays baritone sax with the band in 2009. (Courtesy of Carlos May.)

GRAND MARSHAL. Alcide "Slow Drag" Pavageau (1888–1969) enjoyed a long career, first as a guitarist and then playing the bass. He played with George Lewis and Bunk Johnson in the 1940s, returning to New Orleans in 1961. There, he played with Louis Cottrell, then regularly at Preservation Hall. Seen here in 1950, Slow Drag is dressed as a marshal for the dedication ceremonies of the New Orleans Jazz Museum. (Courtesy of NOPL.)

HALF-FAST. Pete Fountain (1930–) was born Pierre Dewey LaFontaine Jr. His father later changed his own name to Peter Dewey Fountain, and his son followed suit. Diagnosed with a weak-lung condition, Fountain chose to play the clarinet per a doctor's recommendation to play a wind instrument, which would build up his lungs. After learning to play jazz by listening to Benny Goodman recordings, Fountain's first band was the Basin Street Six, founded in 1950. Fountain joined the Lawrence Welk Orchestra in 1954, but soon returned to New Orleans, first playing with the Dukes of Dixieland and then with his own bands. In the late 1960s, Pete founded the Half-Fast Walking Club, a Carnival organization that parades on Mardi Gras. (Courtesy of Robert Avery.)

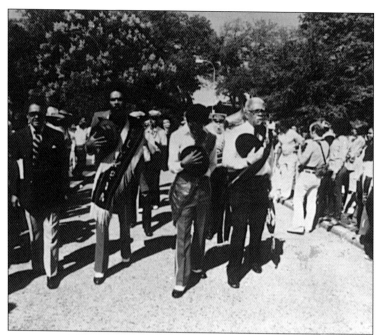

FUNERALS. The custom of providing music for a funeral procession goes back to the mid-1800s. In more recent times, however, jazz funerals have been held not only for individuals but for causes as well. As seen here in 1981, three unidentified parade marshals lead a procession to protest the closure of the New Orleans Marine Hospital. (Courtesy of NHSC.)

MEMORIALS. Sometimes a death in the city moves people to come together for a "proper" New Orleans–style memorial. Such was the case in 2007, when filmmaker and activist Helen Hill was murdered in her Mid-City home. The crime, coming on the heels of the murder of Dinerral Shavers, drummer for the Hot 8 Brass Band, led to an outpouring of emotion in the streets a few weeks later. (Courtesy of Carlos May.)

LIBERTY. Dr. Michael White (1954–), professor of African American Music at Xavier University of Louisiana, is a classically trained clarinetist who was a member of Danny Barker's Fairview Baptist Church Marching Band. Dr. White played with the Young Tuxedo Brass Band, as seen at right in his Tuxedo cap while marching in a jazz funeral in Treme in 1981, also the year in which he founded the Liberty Jazz Band. Having served as guest director for several Jazz at Lincoln Center concerts featuring Wynton Marsalis, he currently records for Basin Street Records. (Both, courtesy of Carlos May.)

BROTHERS. Willie James Humphrey (1900–1994) and Percy Gaston Humphrey (1905–1995) were brothers with extensive jazz careers. Willie played with the Excelsior Band before going to Chicago, where he played with King Oliver. Later, in New Orleans, he played with his brother in the Eureka Band and at Preservation Hall. A regular in the Preservation Hall Jazz Band, Percy led the Eureka Band for more than 30 years. The two are seen playing with the Spirit of New Orleans Band in 1991. Percy is in the front row, second from right, playing trumpet, and Willie is on the far right, playing clarinet. (Courtesy of Carlos May.)

REUNION. Some of the most enjoyable aspects of the annual New Orleans Jazz & Heritage Festival, held from the last weekend of April through the first weekend of May, are the pickup and reunion bands that come together for the fest. This reunion group of the Fairview Baptist band took place at Jazz Fest 2009. (Courtesy of Carlos May.)

SITTING IN. Generations cross over as a young Harry Connick Jr. sits in at Preservation Hall in the early 1970s. The band that evening included, from left to right, Milton Batiste, trumpet; Chester Jones, drums; Harold Dejan, saxophone; Chink Martin, bass; "Sweet Emma" Barrett and Harry Connick Jr., piano; and Emanuel "Manny" Sayles, banjo. (Courtesy of LSM.)

QUARTER TRADITIONAL. Fritzel's European Jazz Pub opened at 733 Bourbon Street in 1969. The house band plays traditional jazz, the term "traditional" being preferred over "Dixieland," which has racial overtones. (Courtesy of Carlos May.)

FUNKIN' IT UP. Brothers Phillip and Keith Frazier, along with Kermit Ruffins and some of their bandmates from Clark Senior High School, founded the Rebirth Brass Band in 1983. Kermit left the band in 1993, but the Rebirth continued to receive critical acclaim and commercial success, appearing in the HBO series *Treme* and winning a Grammy Award in 2012. Pictured here from left to right are (in front) Glen Andrews on trumpet and Vincent Broussard on saxophone; (in back) Keith Frazier on bass drum, Derrick Tabb on snare drum, and Philip Frazier on sousaphone. (Courtesy of Carlos May.)

EDUCATION. The Liberty Brass Band (front) and Rebirth Brass Band (rear) join Dr. Michael White, professor, for a demonstration of second-line parading and dancing at Xavier University in 2010. (Courtesy of Carlos May.)

ALL ABOARD! Local trumpet player Kermit Ruffins (1964–) was a founding member of the Rebirth Brass Band while he was still attending Clark High School in Faubourg Treme. Since leaving Rebirth, Ruffins plays with his jazz quintet, the Barbecue Swingers, seen here at Jazz Fest and at Snug Harbor on Frenchmen Street. Ruffins played himself as a recurring character in the HBO series *Treme*. (Above, courtesy of Derek Bridges; below, Carlos May.)

PUBLICITY. Percy Humphrey poses in the 1960s with the bass drum from the Preservation Hall Jazz Band. Preservation Hall became a home away from home for many older, retired musicians, exposing younger audiences to their talents. (Courtesy of LSM.)

SIDEWALK WARM-UP. This is a more recent incarnation of the Preservation Hall Jazz Band, seen playing on the sidewalk in front of the hall. The band was performing at the memorial parade for clarinetist Jacques Gauthe in 2007. The tradition of hiring a brass band for a funeral has returned with a strong following. When the deceased is one of their own, many musicians will attend the memorial. (Courtesy of Carlos May.)

FOUNDER. Another Fairview Baptist alumnus, sousaphonist Kirk Joseph (1961–) was one of the original members of the Dirty Dozen Brass Band. He now plays with his own band, Kirk Joseph's Backyard Groove. Joseph, who claims inspiration from the late Anthony Lacen, is a good example of the evolution of the New Orleans brass band sound, combining the traditional with elements of funk. (Courtesy of Derek Bridges.)

MENTOR. Anthony "Tuba Fats" Lacen (1950–2004) began busking for tips in the French Quarter and later went on to play with the Young Tuxedo, Doc Paulin's, Onward, Olympia, and Treme Brass Bands. In addition to playing around New Orleans, he toured Europe with his wife, the late Linda Young. (Courtesy of LSM.)

SLOW WALK. The Hot 8 Brass Band leads the way into St. Louis Cemetery No. 3 for the funeral of blogger and activist Ashley Morris, April 11, 2008. The band at a jazz funeral plays slow dirges on the way to the cemetery. Once the deceased is interred, the tempo picks up as the second line celebrates the life of their loved one. (Courtesy of Mark Ghstol.)

TRAGEDY. The Hot 8 Brass Band is a group of younger musicians who came to prominence in post-Katrina New Orleans when they were featured in Spike Lee's documentary about the storm, *When the Levees Broke: A Requiem in Four Acts.* The band's history has been marked by tragedy, as several members have met with violent deaths since the storm. The band is seen here playing Bayou Bougalou, a spring festival held in mid-May along Bayou St. John. (Courtesy of Derek Bridges.)

CENTURY. Pictured above in 1981, Ernest "Doc" Paulin (1907–2007) was a fixture of the New Orleans music scene from the 1920s to the 1990s. Originally from Wallace, Louisiana, north of the city in St. John the Baptist Parish, Paulin moved to the city as a youth. At right, two unidentified members of Paulin's band play for tips at the French Market. Because Paulin was not a member of the musicians' union, he was able to help younger musicians get their start in the business and move to other, better-paying bands. (Above, courtesy of LSM; at right, Carlos May.)

NEXT GENERATION. The To Be Continued (TBC) Brass Band is a splendid example of the latest generation of New Orleans–style brass bands. Borrowing instruments from the George Washington Carver Senior High School band, this group of Seventh and Ninth Ward young men impressed folks at Carver, and the band began playing professionally in 2002. Hurricane Katrina devastated the band, destroying their homes and instruments. Members worked hard to recover from the storm—a recovery that was detailed in the 2010 documentary *From the Mouthpiece and Back*. The band is seen here in 2010, playing a second-line parade for the Valley of Silent Men Social & Pleasure Club. (Courtesy of Derek Bridges.)

ACTIVISM. Since 2006, a group of committed activists and bloggers has sponsored the Rising Tide conference. Billed as a "conference on the future of New Orleans," it features panel discussions, breakout sessions, workshops, and entertainment. The TBC Brass Band performed at Rising Tide 6, held at Xavier University in 2011. (Courtesy of Bart Everson.)

SALUTING THE PAST. Matthew "Fats" Houston (1911–1981) leads the Olympia Brass Band at the funeral of clarinetist George Lewis in 1968. The role of grand marshal is often assumed by an older member of the brass band who is either retired from playing or physically unable to play but can still march. Houston's style and presence earned the band a role in the James Bond film *Live and Let Die*. (Courtesy of LSM.)

OLYMPIA. While Fats Houston might have been the public face of the Olympia Brass Band, its leader was Harold Dejan (1909–2002). When interest in traditional jazz and brass bands was at an all-time low in the late 1960s to early 1970s, Dejan's Olympia was a forceful and visible presence that inspired the next generation of players. (Courtesy of NOPL.)

Shorty. A very young Troy "Trombone Shorty" Andrews marches in a second-line parade around the fairgrounds at Jazz Fest in 1994. In addition to the acts booked for the various Jazz Fest stages, the festival schedules daily second-line parades featuring brass bands and social-aid club marching bands. (Courtesy of Carlos May.)

All on a Mardi Gras Day. Carlos "Froggy" May plays trombone with the Storyville Stompers Brass Band and other friends in the Bywater neighborhood of New Orleans on Carnival Day in 2009. (Courtesy of Carlos May.)

COMMUNITY. WWOZ, founded by Brock brothers Walter and Jerry, took to the airwaves of New Orleans on December 4, 1980. The 4,000-watt station (90.7 FM, streaming at wwoz.org) is a community-oriented, nonprofit entity offering jazz programming as well as R&B, Celtic, Latin, ethnic, and world music. The station also does live broadcasts of local music events, particularly the New Orleans Jazz & Heritage festival. WWOZ DJs Tom Morgan and Valerie "the Problem Child" Kacprzak are shown here, broadcasting during Jazz Fest 2007. (Courtesy of Carlos May.)

STOMPIN'. The Storyville Stompers lead off a second-line parade on a sunny day at Jackson Square to open French Quarter Fest in April 2010. French Quarter Fest is different from the larger Jazz & Heritage Festival in that all the music is free; musicians perform at various stages set up around the French Quarter. Restaurants and other food vendors set up in Jackson Square and in Woldenberg Park along the river. Sponsors and sales of food help fund the annual event, held in mid-April. (Courtesy of Carlos May.)

COFFINS. Musician, author, and photographer Louis Maistros sings at a book reading/signing in 2009 for his novel *The Sound of Building Coffins* at Octavia Books, located on Laurel Street in Uptown. Set in the Storyville era, *Coffins* is historical fiction narrative with a unique twist. A fictional Buddy Bolden is one of the lead characters in this fascinating look at turn-of-the-century New Orleans. (Courtesy of Carlos May.)

Jazz Camp. The mission of the New Orleans Traditional Jazz Camp, founded by Leslie Cooper, Banu Gibson, and Anita Hemeter, is to bring together musicians from around the world who are interested in learning to play traditional New Orleans jazz or who want to continue developing their skills. Students come to New Orleans for a week to study under jazz masters before performing at various clubs and, finally, at Preservation Hall by the end of the week. Here, students from the 2013 camp show off their talents at Palm Court Jazz Café. (Courtesy of Carlos May.)

Boswell Homage. From left to right, Holley Bendtsen, Yvette Voelker, and Debbie Davis are known as the Pfister Sisters. The trio has been singing traditional jazz standards in the style of the 1940s sister act from New Orleans, the Boswell Sisters, since 1979. The "sisters" are shown here in 2007, singing at the Cabildo celebration for the centennial of Connee Boswell's birth. (Courtesy of Carlos May.)

INFLUENCE. "Uncle Lionel" Batiste (1932–2012) was the bass drummer for the Treme Brass Band, as well as an inspiration and role model to several generations of New Orleans jazz musicians. As such, Batiste was nominated as king of the Krewe de Vieux parade for Carnival 2003 and appeared in the pilot episode of the HBO series *Treme*. (Courtesy of Carlos May.)

GOIN' HOME. Unidentified members of the Algiers Brass Band march in a jazz funeral procession in the late 1980s. (Courtesy of Carlos May.)

PRESERVATION ON PARADE. While the original incarnations of the Preservation Hall Jazz Band consisted of mostly older musicians who stayed at the hall, the current band gets out and about. Here, the band winds its way through the crowd gathered on Frenchmen Street for Carnival Day, February 12, 2013, breathing an incredible amount of new life into a New Orleans institution. (Courtesy of Carlos May.)

Six

MODERN JAZZ

It is not all about the traditional in New Orleans. Many players eschewed Dixieland from the start of their careers, opting to play Chicago-style or New York–style jazz at home. Classically trained musicians, many of whom studied away from New Orleans, came back wanting to create a different kind of jazz from what Bolden, Oliver, and Bonano played. Ellis Marsalis Jr. is a great example of this trend, particularly because he influenced his sons to follow his modernist path. Because he is such a skilled teacher and mentor, Marsalis helped nurture the careers of younger modern jazz musicians, particularly through the jazz programs at the University of New Orleans. Even modernists know their roots, though, as when Wynton Marsalis plays strains of "Saints" in a video to honor the appearance of the New Orleans Saints at the Super Bowl or when Donald Harrison Jr. dons his "suit of pretty" and assumes control of the Congo Nation Mardi Gras Indian tribe as the "Big Chief."

PATRIARCH. Ellis Marsalis Jr. (1934–) began playing the saxophone as a child, switching to piano in high school. He has played with Cannonball Adderley, Al Hirt, and Eddie Harris, but he never specialized in Dixieland. A true teacher, Ellis is affiliated with the New Orleans Center for Creative Arts (NOCCA), University of New Orleans, and Xavier University of Louisiana. Marsalis and his wife, Delores, have six sons, four of whom are jazz musicians. (Courtesy of USMC.)

FUSION. Tony Dagradi founded Astral Project in 1978. The quartet consists of Dagradi on sax, Johnny Vidacovich on drums, James Singleton on bass, and Steve Masakowski on guitar. The group is seen here in 2010 playing at the French Quarter Fest. (Courtesy of Derek Bridges.)

MODERN MAESTRO. Wynton Learson Marsalis (1961–) has had the most commercial success of the family. An alumnus of the Fairview Baptist Band, Marsalis took a more modern direction with his music. He cofounded the jazz program at Lincoln Center in New York and has won nine Grammy Awards. He also gave a moving musical and poetic tribute to the New Orleans Saints during the pregame ceremonies for Super Bowl XLIV. (Courtesy of Darlene Susco.)

TONIGHT. Branford Marsalis (1960–) is also a Fairview alumnus. Marsalis toured Europe with Lionel Hampton and Clark Terry while a college student in 1980. He worked with Sting on his solo "The Dream of Blue Turtles" in 1985. Branford was leader of the Tonight Show Band from 1992 to 1995. Recently, in 2012, he recorded "Four MFs Playin' Tunes" on high-grade vinyl. Also released on CD and in digital form, it was named Apple iTunes 2012 Instrumental Album of the Year. (Courtesy of LOC.)

ASTRAL DRUMS. Johnny Vidacovich has been the drummer for Astral Project since the early 1970s and has played with a wide range of musicians, including Bobby McFerrin, Professor Longhair, James Booker, and Mose Allison. He is also part of The Trio, playing a regular gig at the Maple Leaf Bar with George Porter Jr. Vidacovich has also served on the faculty of Loyola University's School of Music. (Courtesy of Lisa Hill.)

FATHER-DAUGHTER. Guitarist Steve Masakowski holds the Coca-Cola endowed chair of jazz studies at the University of New Orleans. Masakowski has played guitar with many local legends, including Alvin "Red" Tyler, Ellis Marsalis, Danny Barker, Earl Turbinton, and James Black. He also performs with his daughter Sasha, who went to high school at NOCCA. Sasha then studied under Ellis Marsalis at UNO. She released her first CD in 2009 and tours regularly. Steve and Sasha are seen here at the Old Algiers Riverfest in 2012. (Courtesy of Carlos May.)

CROONER. Wynton Marsalis and Harry Connick Jr. both persuaded Jeremy Davenport to move to New Orleans in the mid-1990s, where he could study under Ellis Marsalis. After completing his studies at the University of New Orleans, he joined the Harry Connick Jr. Big Band, touring with the group for six years. He returned to New Orleans, playing various clubs, and now he has his own club, the Davenport Lounge, in the Ritz-Carlton Hotel on Canal Street. (Both, courtesy of Basin Street Records.)

HARD BOP. A childhood friend of Wynton Marsalis, Terence Blanchard (1962–) studied under Ellis Marsalis Jr. at NOCCA and eventually replaced Wynton as trumpet player in the Jazz Messengers. As artistic director at the Thelonious Monk Institute of Jazz at the University of Southern California, he successfully lobbied the institute to move to Loyola University of New Orleans, post Katrina. Blanchard plays trumpet in the "hard bop" tradition. (Courtesy of NOPL.)

Shorty. Troy Andrews (1986–) plays trombone and trumpet. His older brother James is a bandleader. At the age of six, Troy began playing trombone, which is where he got his nickname, "Trombone Shorty." Andrews attended NOCCA and was a member of the Stooges Brass Band. He joined Lenny Kravitz's horn section in 2005 on Kravitz's world tour that year. Andrews and his band, Orleans Avenue, recorded their first CD, *Orleans and Claiborne*, in 2005, followed by the critically acclaimed *Backatown*, which hit Billboard's Contemporary Jazz Chart at No. 1 and stayed there for nine weeks. Andrews had a recurring role as himself in the HBO series *Treme* and has received numerous awards for his community work and service through the Trombone Shorty Foundation. (Courtesy of Derek Bridges.)

COMMANDER-IN-CHIEF PERFORMANCE.
Trombone Shorty (center background)
looks on as President Obama
sings "Sweet Home Chicago" with
B.B. King during a White House
performance on February 21, 2012.
(Courtesy of the White House.)

FESTIN'. Troy Andrews has replaced
the Neville Brothers as the final act
on the second Sunday of the New
Orleans Jazz & Heritage Festival.
This passing of the torch from
one generation of New Orleans
greats to another demonstrates the
robustness of modern New Orleans
jazz. (Courtesy of Carlos May.)

NOJO. Irvin Mayfield Jr. grew up in the Upper Ninth Ward and went to high school at NOCCA. Mayfield declined a scholarship to study at the Julliard School of Music, opting instead to study under Ellis Marsalis at the University of New Orleans. Mayfield is a cofounder of Los Hombres Calientes, a Basin Street Records group, as well as the artistic director of the New Orleans Jazz Orchestra (NOJO). He also performs at his club, Irvin Mayfield's Jazz Playhouse, at the Royal Sonesta Hotel on Bourbon Street. (At left, courtesy Basin Street Records; below, Derek Bridges.)

AFRO-CUBAN. Led by Irvin Mayfield on trumpet and Bill Summers on percussion, Los Hombres Calientes adds a Latin flavor to classic New Orleans jazz, giving audiences a spicy and bouncy mix of power. Summers brings his experience playing with jazz greats Quincy Jones and Herbie Hancock to blend with Mayfield's horn. (Courtesy of Basin Street Records.)

PRESERVATIONIST. Shannon Powell first played professionally in Danny Barker's band, the Jazzhounds, in 1976. He later played for six years with the Harry Connick Jr. Big Band, as well as a list of jazz legends, including Ellis Marsalis, Willie Metcalf Jr., Branford Marsalis, Wynton Marsalis & the Lincoln Center Jazz Orchestra, Diana Krall, Earl King, Dr. John, Marcus Roberts, John Scofield, Jason Marsalis, Leroy Jones, Nicholas Payton, and Donald Harrison Jr. Currently, he is a member of the Preservation Hall Jazz Band. (Courtesy of Carlos May.)

FAMILY. Ingrid Lucia joined her family's band, the Flying Nutrinos, at an early age, playing drums and singing. Her parents left the band in the 1990s, and she took over its leadership. Lucia now fronts for the band as it records and plays festivals, such as the New Orleans Jazz & Heritage Festival. (Courtesy of Carlos May.)

COMMUNITY. As the younger brother of Wynton and Branford, trombonist Delfeayo Marsalis is a graduate of the Berklee College of Music and the founder of the Uptown Music Theater in New Orleans, whose mission is "community unity." (Both, courtesy of Carlos May.)

ORPHEUS RISING. Harry Connick Jr. (1967–) is the son of former Orleans Parish district attorney Harry Connick Sr. At the age of nine, he performed with the New Orleans Symphony Orchestra. As a teen, Connick was mentored by Ellis Marsalis Sr. and James Booker at NOCCA. After high school and a brief period of studying at Loyola University, Connick moved to New York, where he studied at the Manhattan School of Music and was signed by Columbia Records. After recording his debut album and a follow-up, he received the opportunity to record the sound track for Rob Reiner's 1989 movie *When Harry Met Sally*. Connick made his acting debut in 1990, in the film *Memphis Belle*, and has enjoyed critical acclaim as both an actor and a musician. Locally, Connick is lauded for founding the Krewe of Orpheus Carnival organization, whose signature float is the Leviathan. Orpheus, which parades on Lundi Gras, has rapidly grown in popularity and is regarded as a "super-krewe." Connick has also been very active in the recovery of the Lower Ninth Ward neighborhood in the wake of Hurricane Katrina. (Courtesy of Wendy Piersall.)

NOUVEAU SWING. A graduate of NOCCA, saxophonist Donald Harrison Jr. is the creator of the "nouveau swing" style and the Big Chief of the Congo Nation Mardi Gras Indian tribe, which keeps alive the secret traditions of Congo Square. The Donald Harrison Electric Band has charted on Billboard, and Harrison has appeared as himself in numerous episodes of the HBO series *Treme*. Many believe the *Treme* characters of Albert and Delmond Lambreaux are based on Harrison and his father, Donald Sr. (Courtesy of Derek Bridges.)

FEST FOUNDER. Already well known as the producer of the Newport Jazz Festival in Rhode Island, George Wein was tapped by the New Orleans Jazz & Heritage Foundation to produce a large-scale festival for the city. Wein's company, Festival Productions, Inc., formed a local affiliate, Festival Productions, Inc., New Orleans, to produce the event under contract from the foundation. (Courtesy of Carlos May.)

FEST DADDY. Quint Davis was working as an intern at the Hogan Jazz Archive of Tulane University when he was recommended to George Wein to help produce the 1970 Jazz Fest. Davis stayed with Festival Productions, Inc., New Orleans, assuming day-to-day operations. Davis negotiated the deal to move the festival from its original location in Congo Square to the New Orleans Fair Grounds for the 1972 event. (Courtesy of Derek Bridges.)

Jazz Master. As the youngest of Ellis Marsalis Jr.'s performing sons, Jason Marsalis played his first professional gig with his father at the age of 12 before studying classical percussion at Loyola University of New Orleans. In addition to performing modern jazz with his father and brothers, Jason has played with numerous New Orleans legends and current headliners, including traditional jazz as a sideman for Dr. Michael White. (Courtesy of Carlos May.)

Trombone Rock. Trombonists Mark Mullins and Craig Klein played together in Harry Connick Jr.'s Big Band for over a decade. They formed Bonerama in 1998, playing jazz and rock tunes with a trombone front. Known as "The Bones," they are, from left to right, Craig Klein, Mark Mullins, Steve Suter, and Rick Trolsen. Original "Bone" Brian O'Neill passed away in 2005, while Suter and Trolsen left the band in 2009. Bonerama has since added Greg Hicks and now plays with three trombones up front. They are seen here at the New Orleans Jazz and Heritage Festival in 2006. (Courtesy of Carlos May.)

MARIGNY TRIANGLE. Faubourg Marigny is the second-oldest neighborhood in the city. Frenchmen Street, just on the downriver side of the French Quarter, is home to a number of music clubs offering both modern and traditional jazz, as well as other types of bands. Three Muses, on the 500 block of Frenchmen, is a wonderful place for happy hour or a light dinner, followed by some great music. (Both, author's collection.)

INTERNET. Swedish-born Theresa Andersson came to New Orleans in 1990 as part of Anders Osborne's band and never left. She has played with many New Orleans maestros, including The Meters and Allen Toussaint. Andersson is a new-media pioneer; her song, "Na Na Na," has over 1.5 million views on YouTube, leading the way into the world of digital delivery. (Courtesy of Basin Street Records.)

TREME STAR. Located in the 500 block of Frenchmen Street, right next to Three Muses, is the Blue Nile. The club became a regular location for the HBO series *Treme*, with real-life legend Kermit Ruffins playing there, as well as fictional journeyman trombonist Antoine Baptiste, played by actor Wendell Pierce. (Author's collection.)

HIP-ROCK. A product of school bands in New Orleans, Shamarr Allen attended the Louis "Satchmo" Armstrong Jazz Camp as a teen, where his talents were recognized by several educators. At 13, he was invited to play with the University of Pittsburgh Orchestra, and at 16, he appeared at Carnegie Hall with the Mahogany Brass Band. Now leading his own band, the Underdawgs, Allen plays local gigs and festivals, as well as international tours. His style is an incredible fusion of jazz, hip-hop, and rock, which Allen calls "hip-rock." (Courtesy of JonGunnar Gylfason.)

COMPOSER. Allen Toussaint (1938–) is best known as a songwriter and producer. Toussaint's music crosses over several styles of jazz, R&B, and rock. Many artists have had great commercial success covering Toussaint's songs, most notably Glenn Campbell, who did "Southern Nights" in 1977, riding it to the No. 1 spot on three charts: Pop, Adult Contemporary, and Country. Toussaint has produced artists as diverse as Robert Palmer, Elvis Costello, The Band, Paul McCartney, and many local musicians. (Courtesy of Carl Lender.)

GOING ON. Buried with his father, Anthony, and his mother, Angelina, Louis Prima's tomb in Metairie Cemetery bears an epitaph fitting of all jazz music that originates in New Orleans: "When the end comes, I know, they'll say, 'just a gigolo,' as life goes on, without me." Life and music do indeed go on in New Orleans. Yesterday's child prodigies are today's mentors. As long as the heritage of how we got to this point is remembered, life will go on well. (Author's collection.)

Discover Thousands of Local History Books Featuring Millions of Vintage Images

Arcadia Publishing, the leading local history publisher in the United States, is committed to making history accessible and meaningful through publishing books that celebrate and preserve the heritage of America's people and places.

Find more books like this at
www.arcadiapublishing.com

Search for your hometown history, your old stomping grounds, and even your favorite sports team.

Consistent with our mission to preserve history on a local level, this book was printed in South Carolina on American-made paper and manufactured entirely in the United States. Products carrying the accredited Forest Stewardship Council (FSC) label are printed on 100 percent FSC-certified paper.

MADE IN THE USA